Hebrew Coloring Book
Color the Alef Bet

Copyright © 2020 Sharon Asher

All rights reserved.

No part of this book may be copied and/or altered and/or distributed and/or reproduced in any form or by any electronic or mechanical means, including but not limited to information storage and retrieval systems, without express permission in writing from the author.

ISBN-13: 978-1-951462-07-9

אבטיח

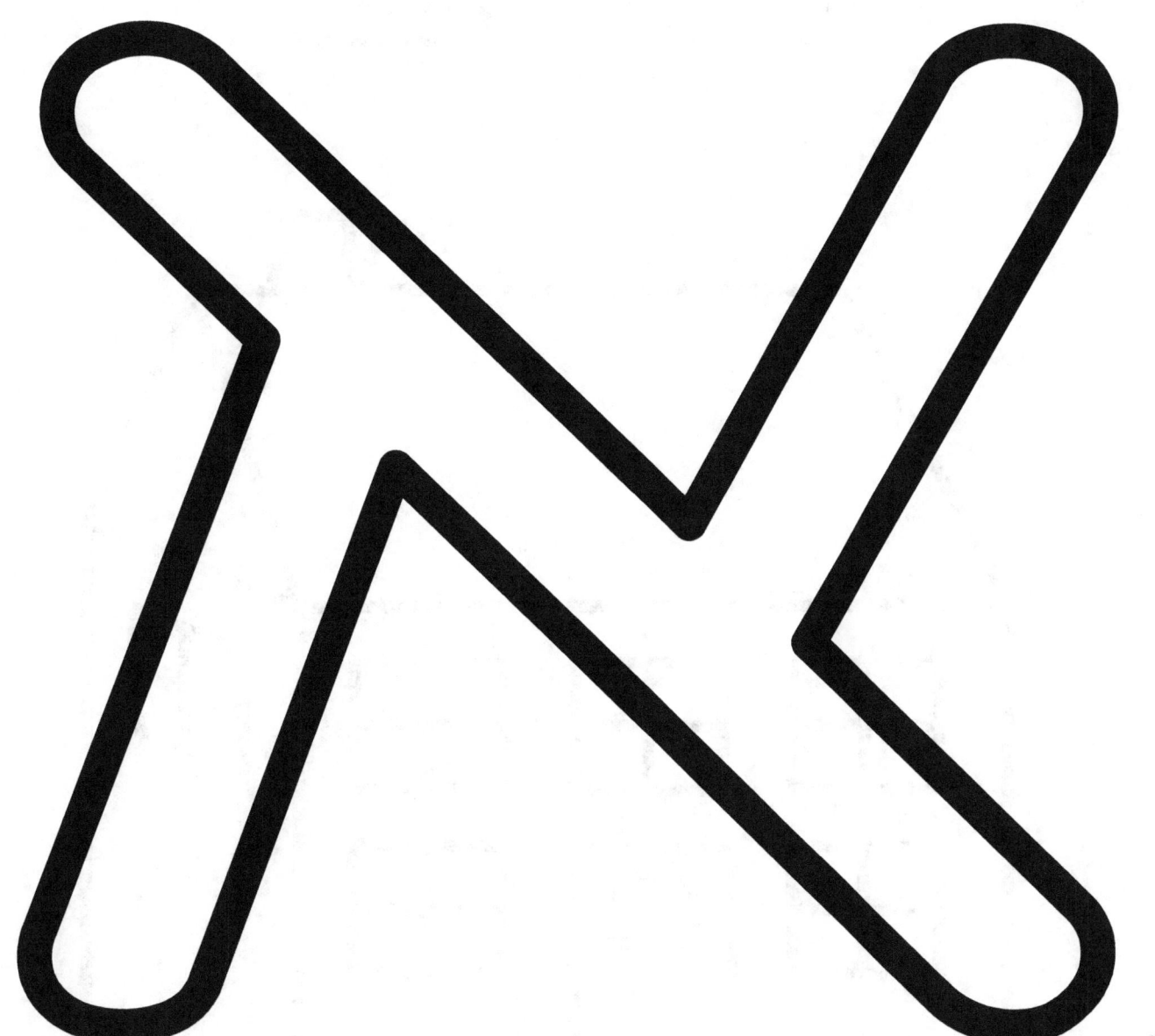

בִּית

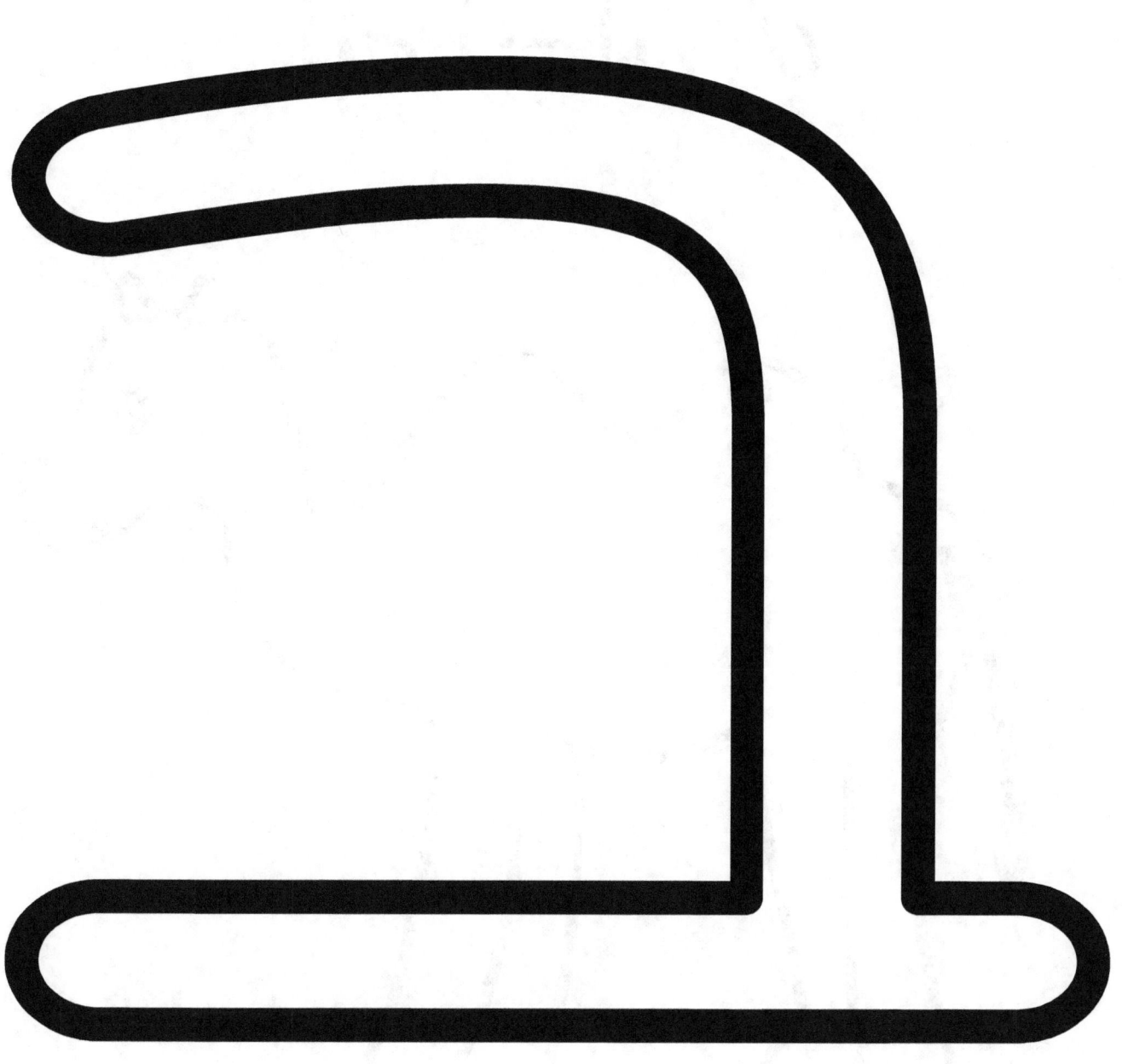

גמל

ว

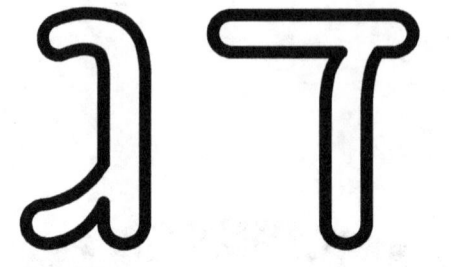

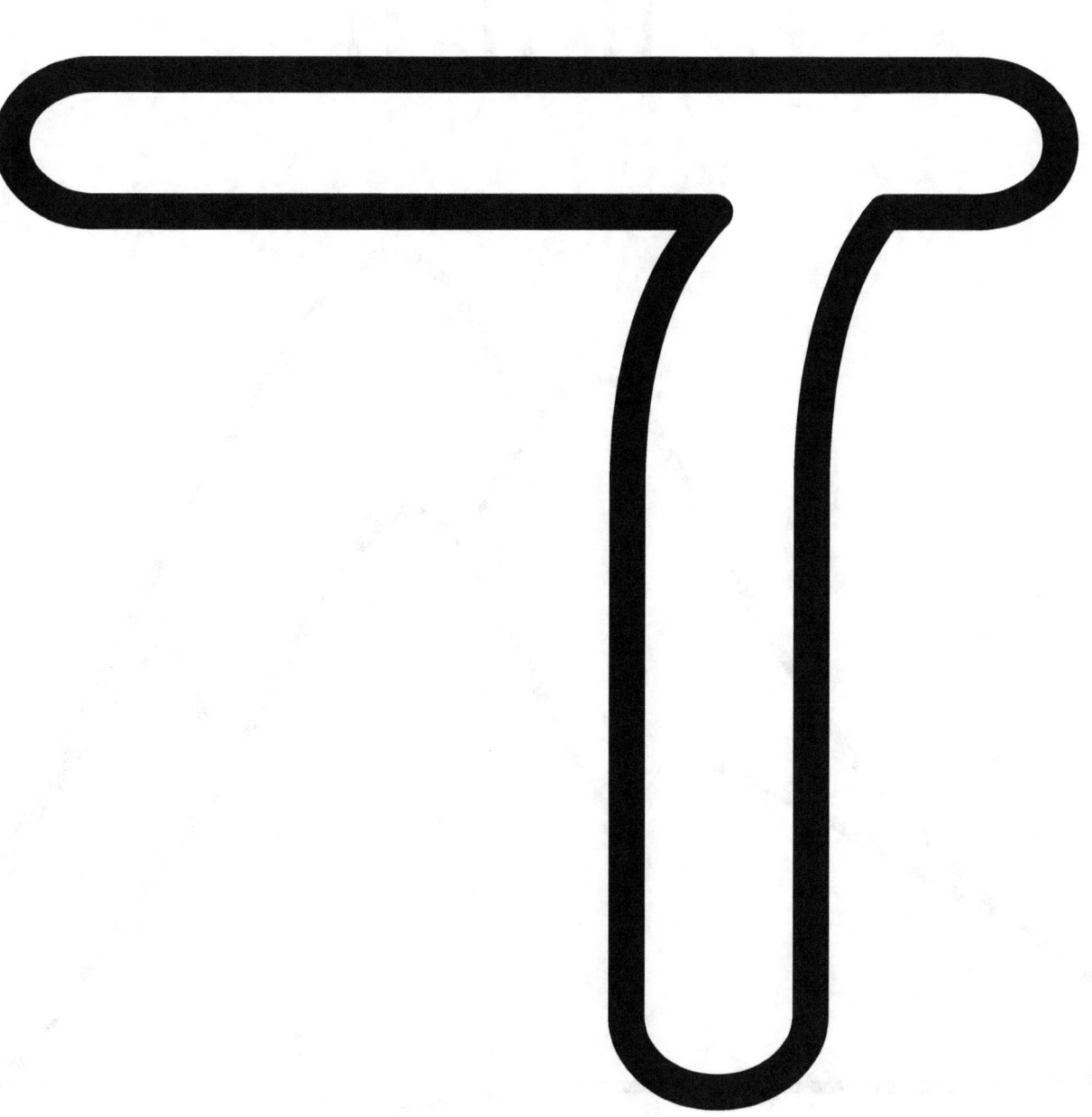

הר

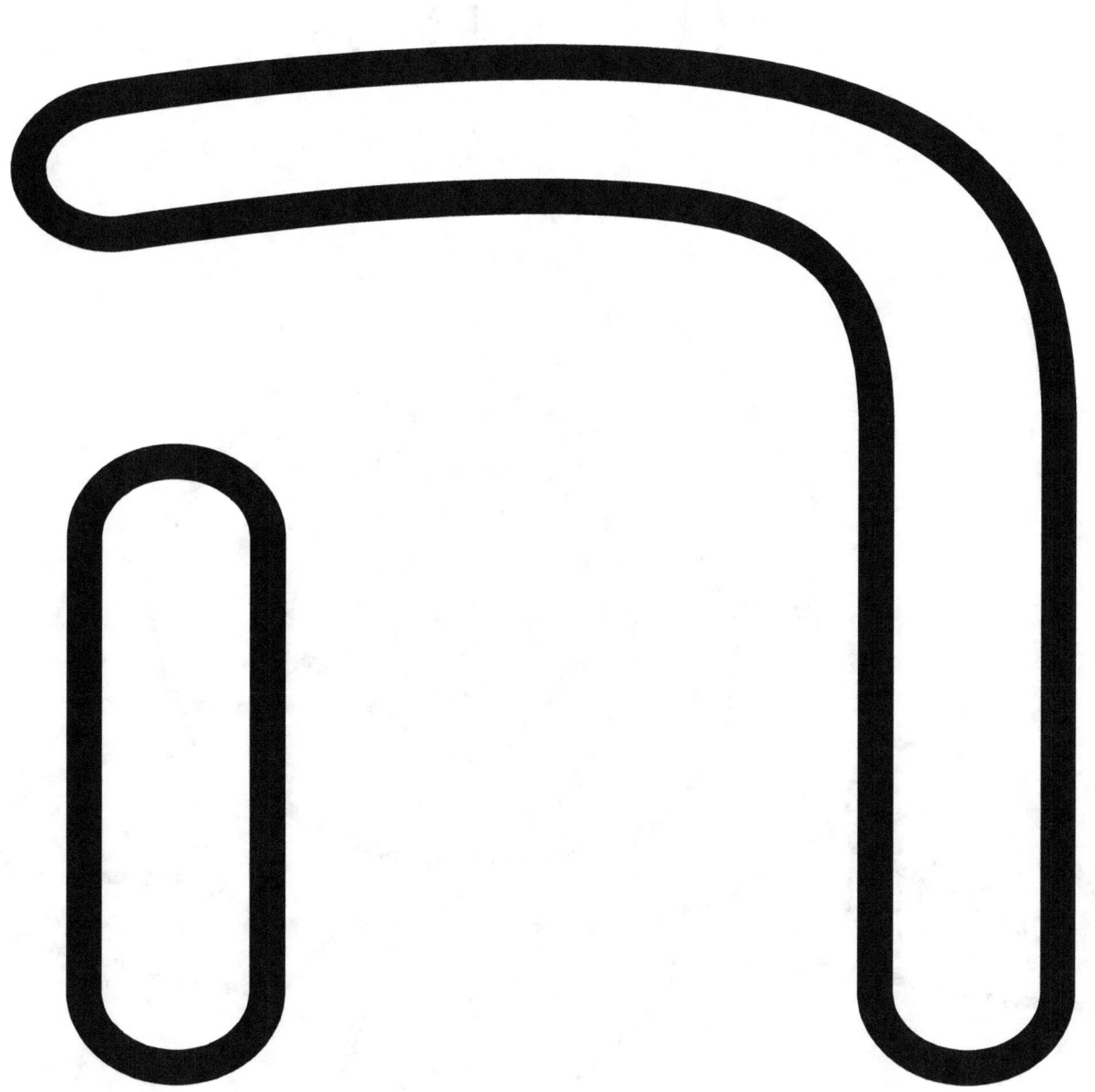

ורד

זיתים

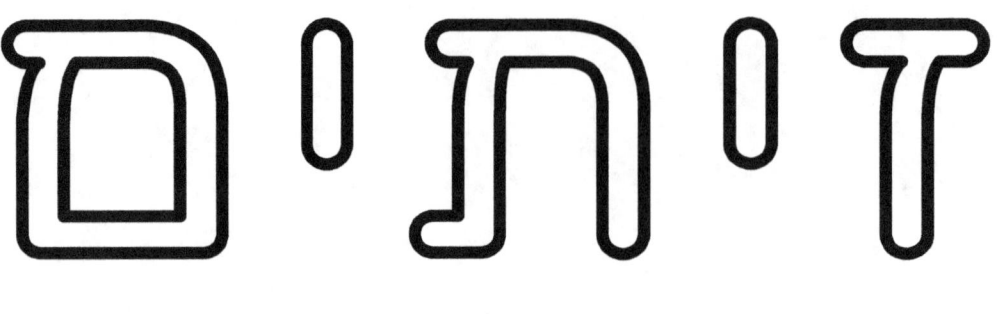

T

חיפושית

ה

טרקטור

U

ירח

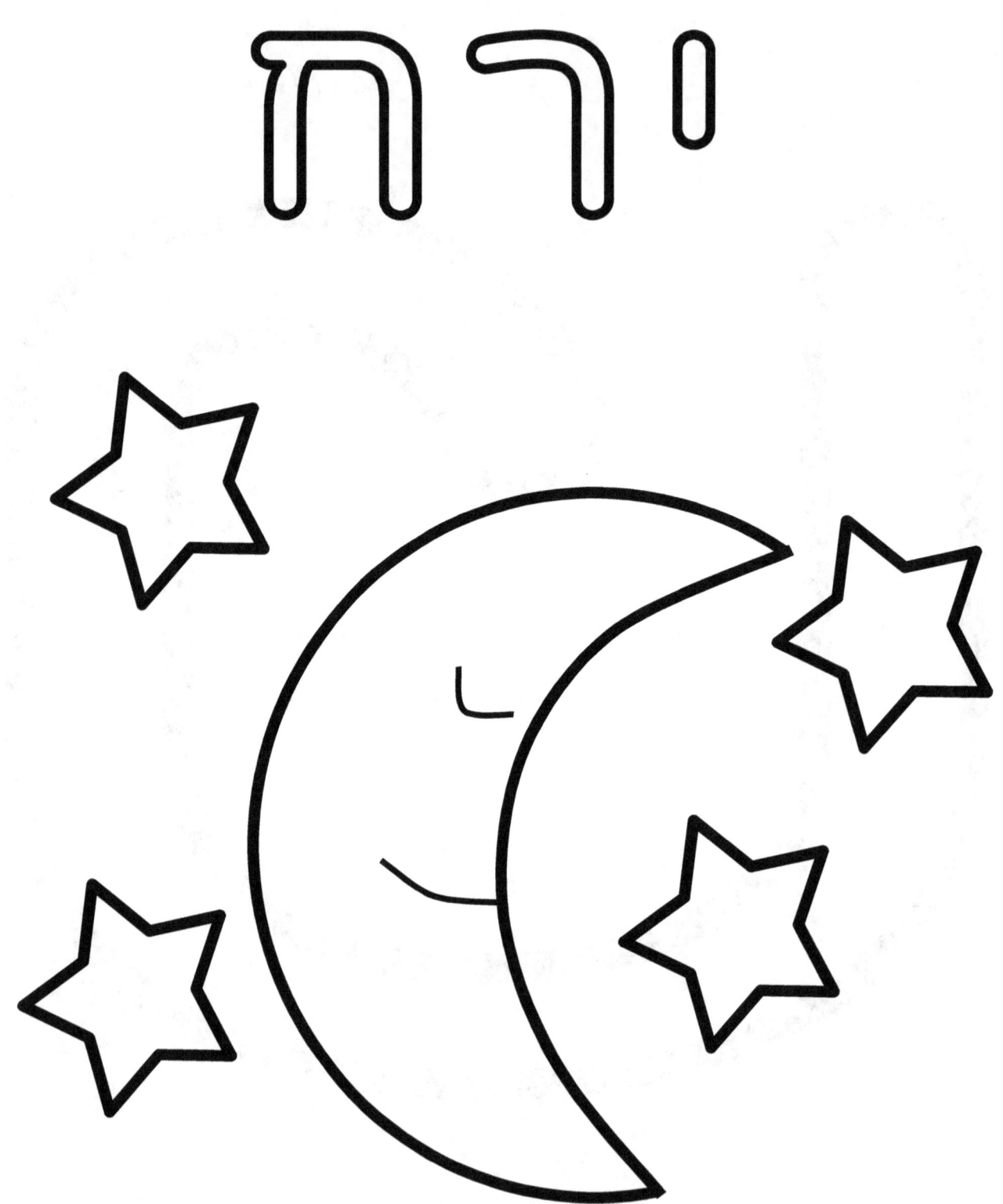

כפפה

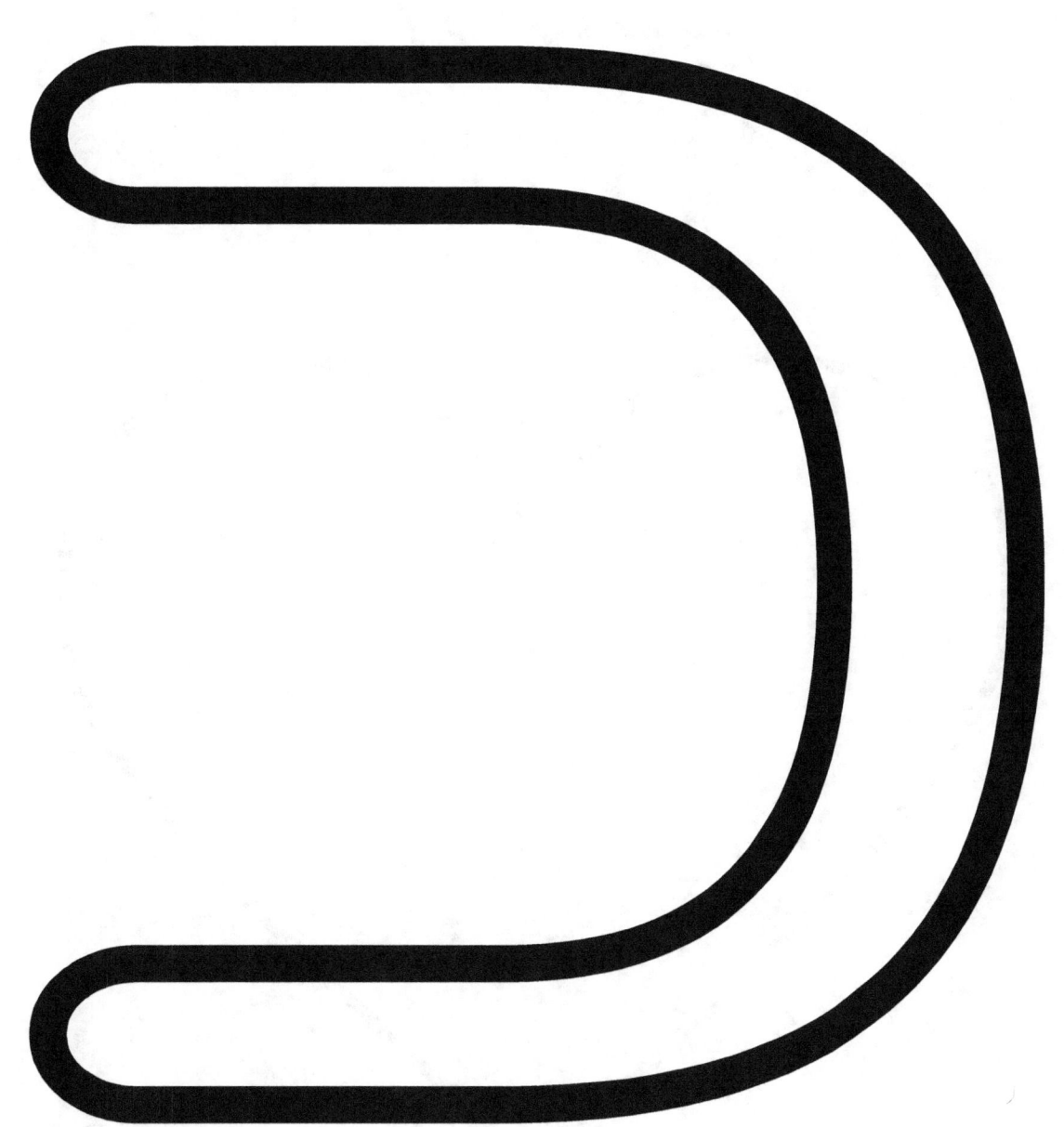

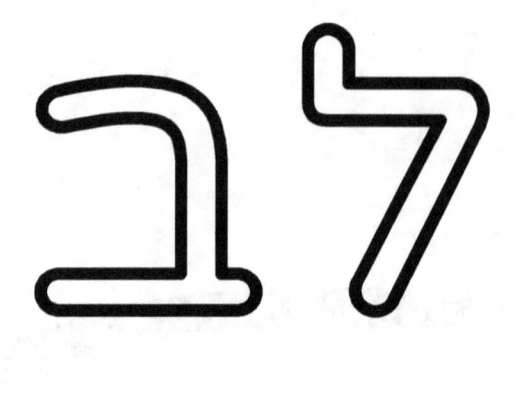

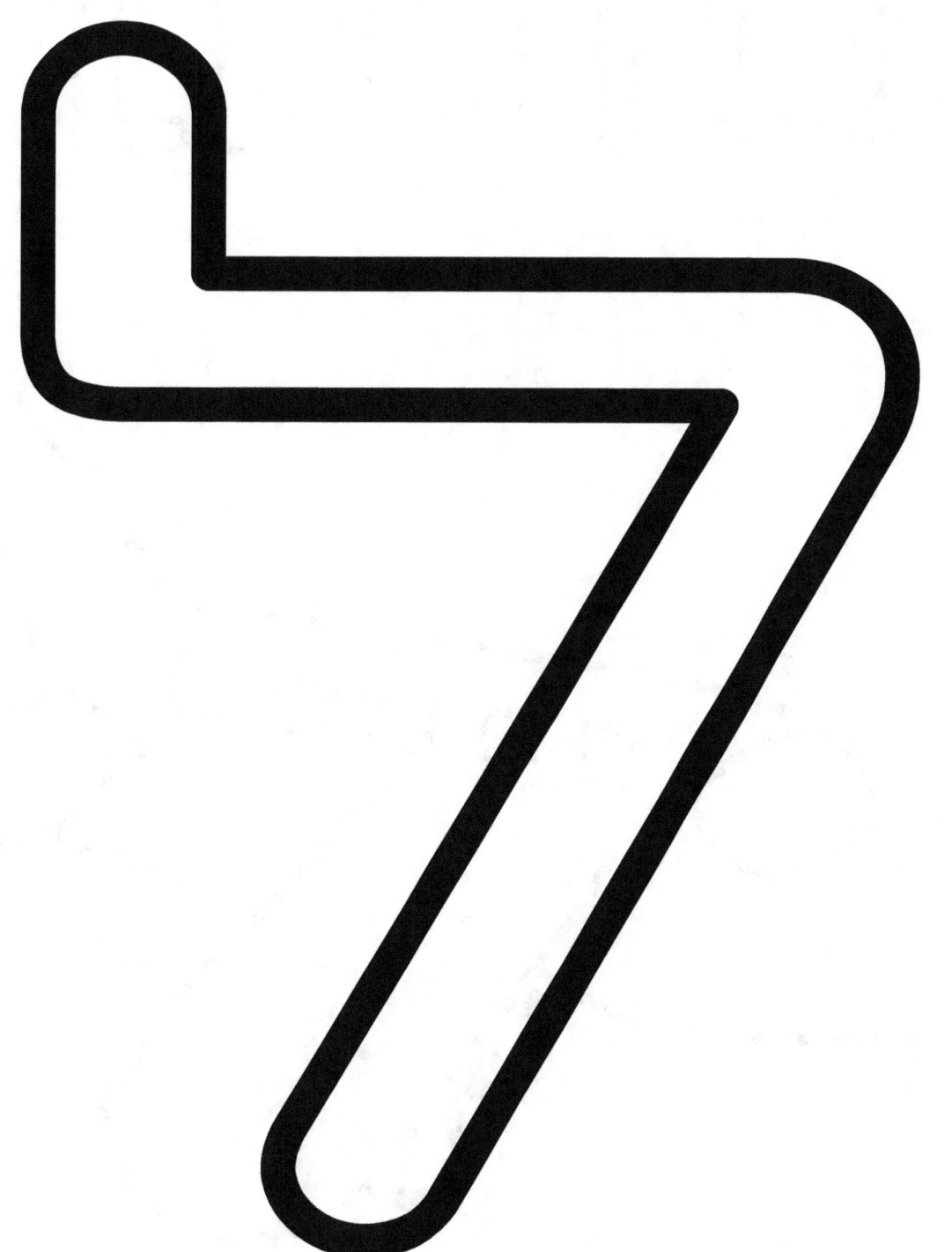

מטוס

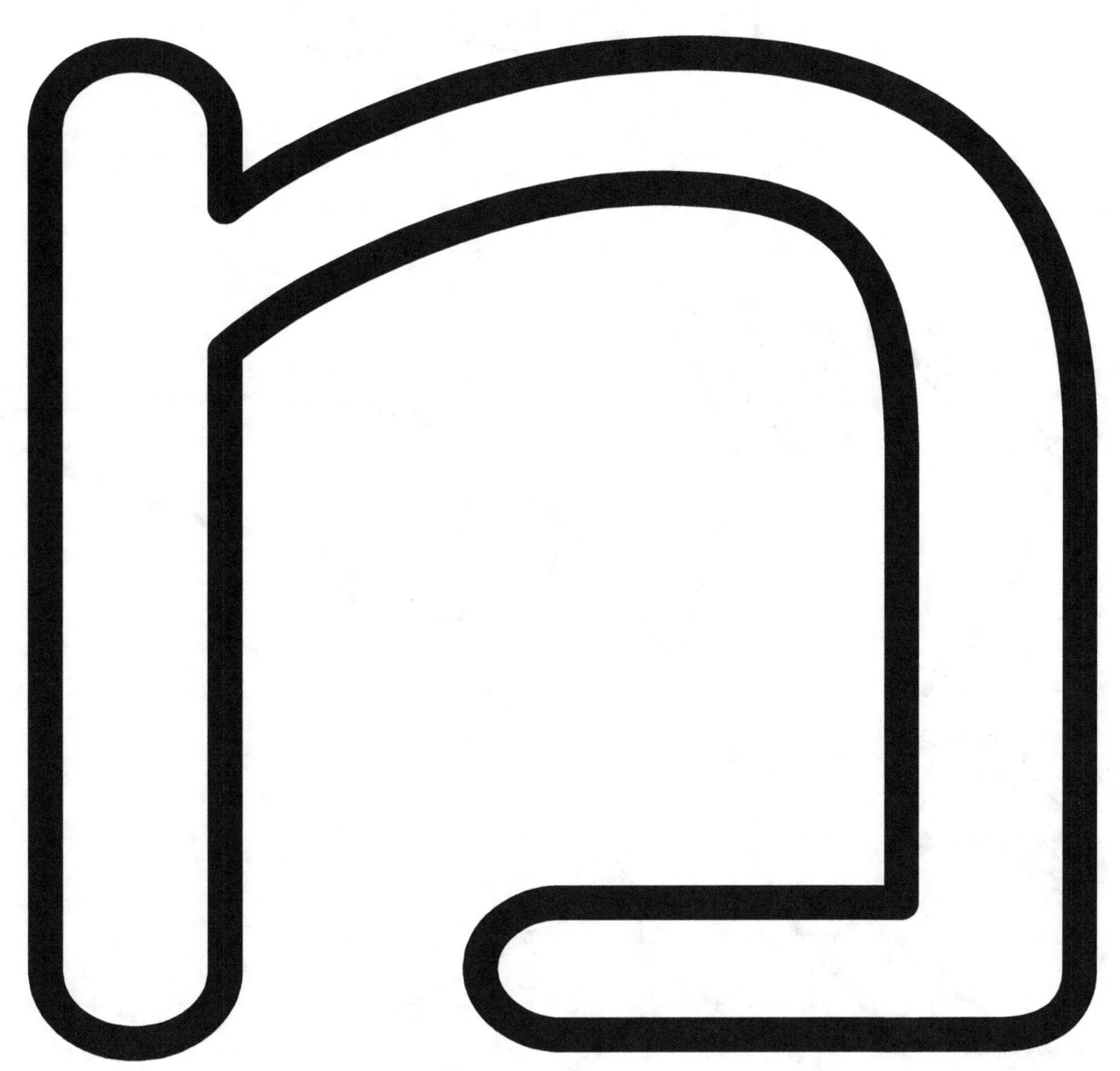

נשר

J

סנדל

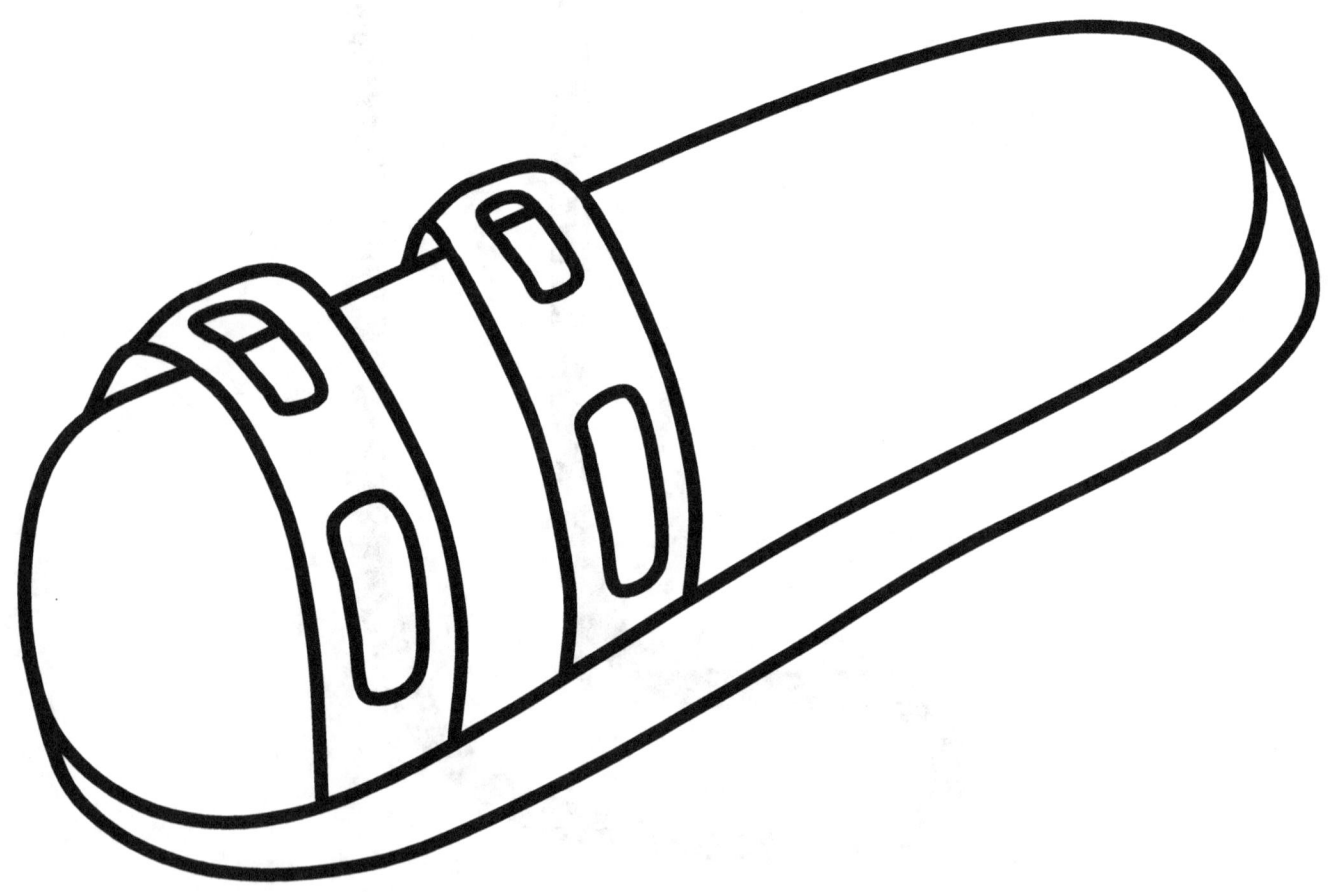

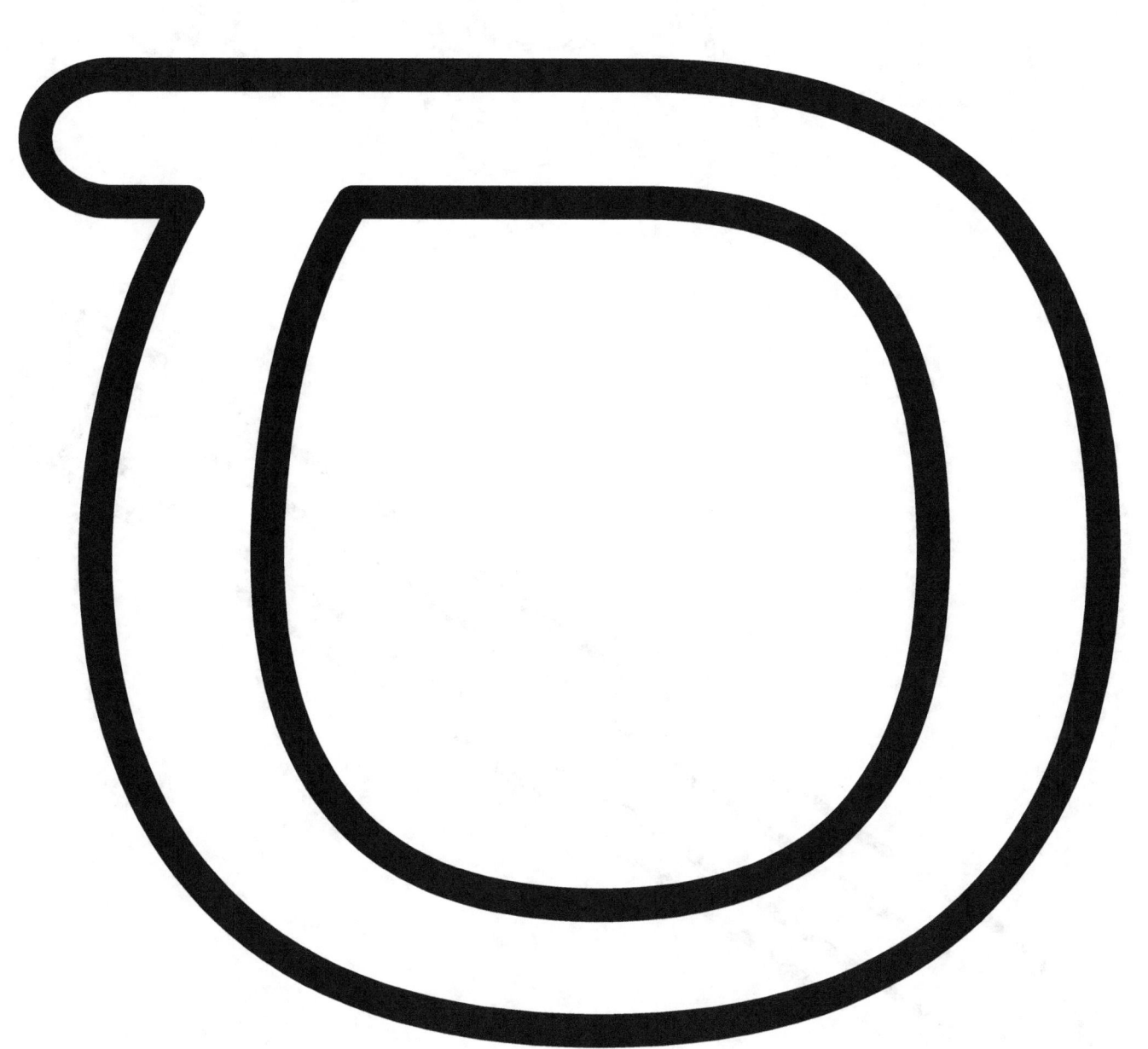

עיפרון

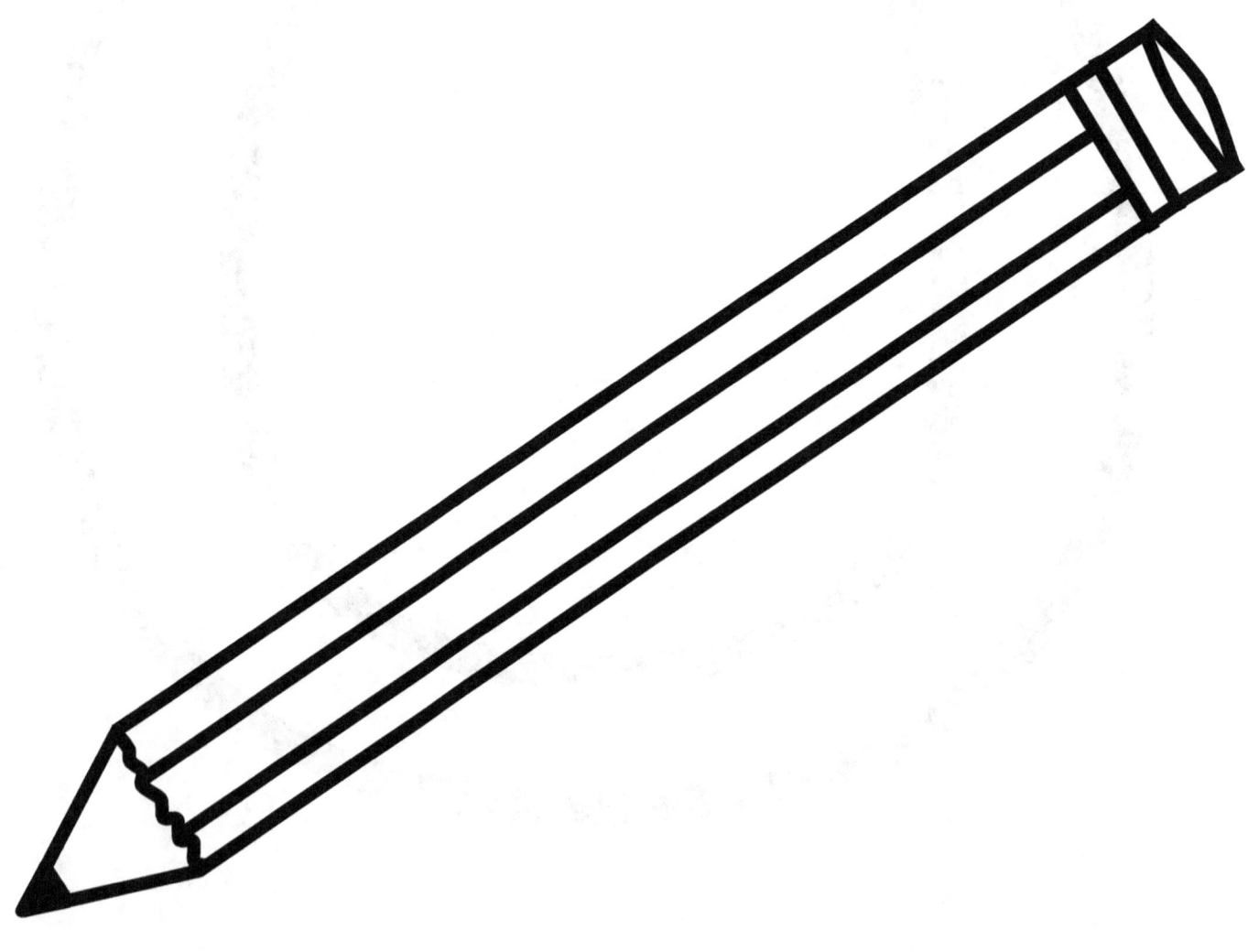

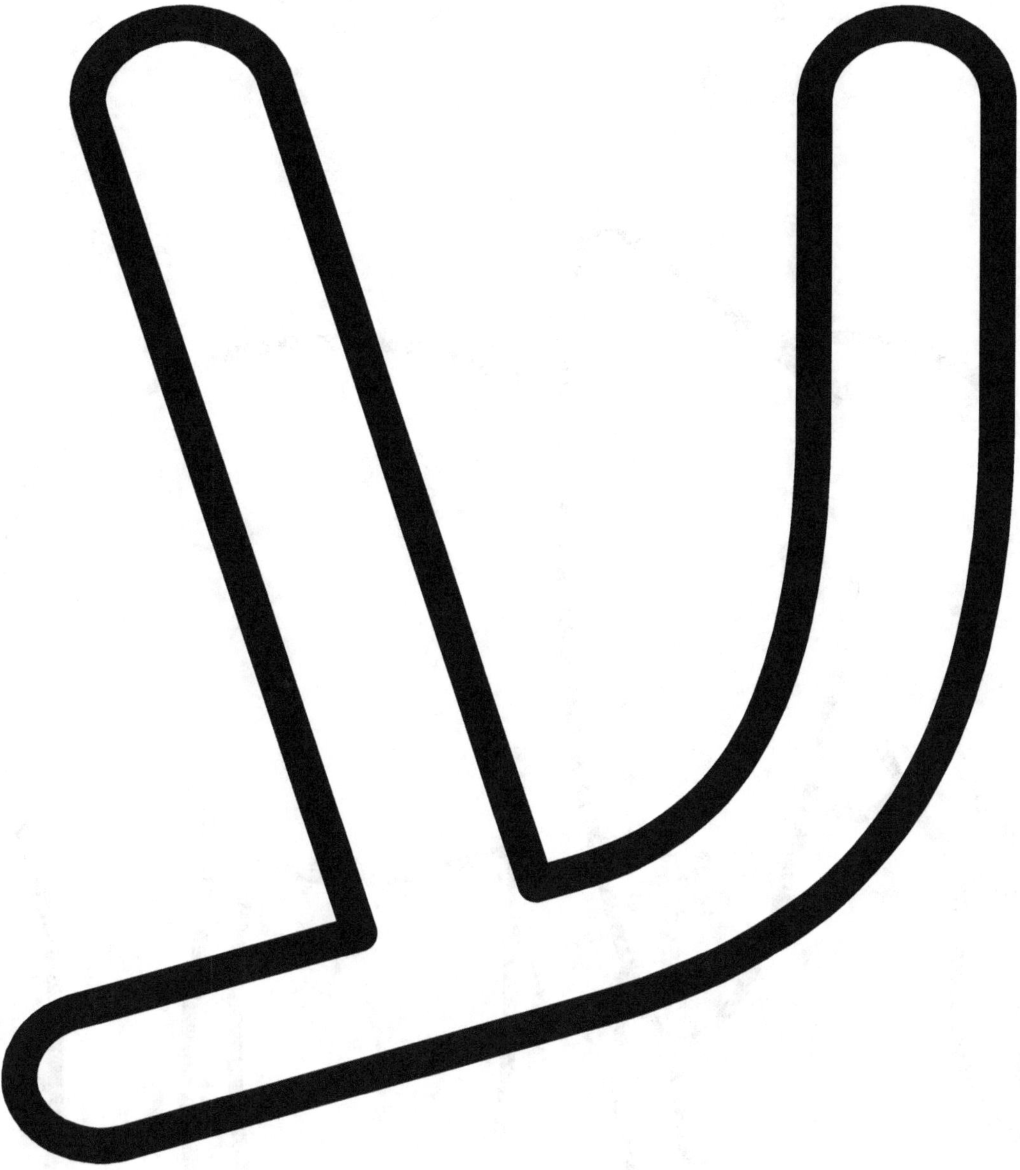
ע

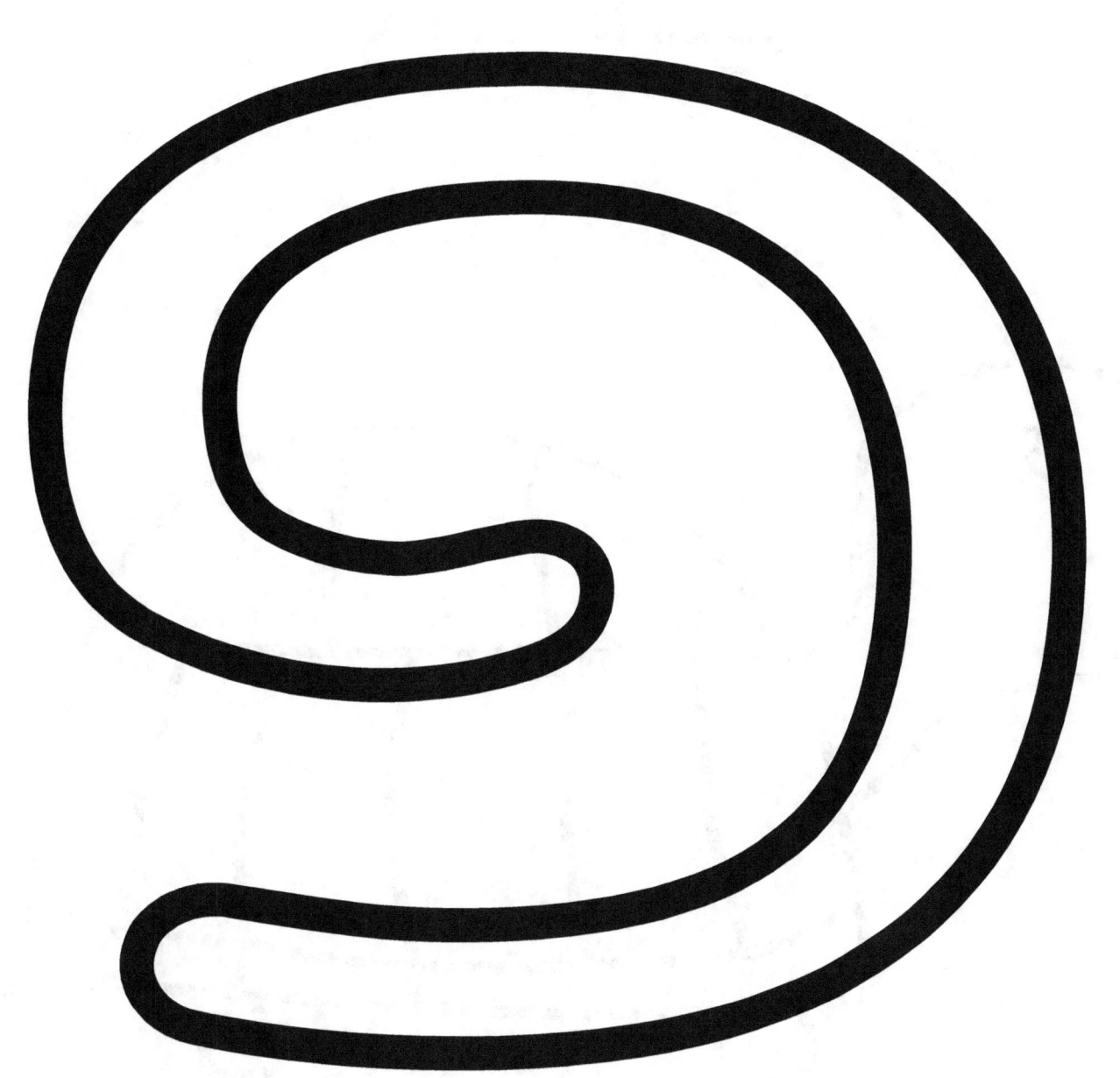

צב

קשת

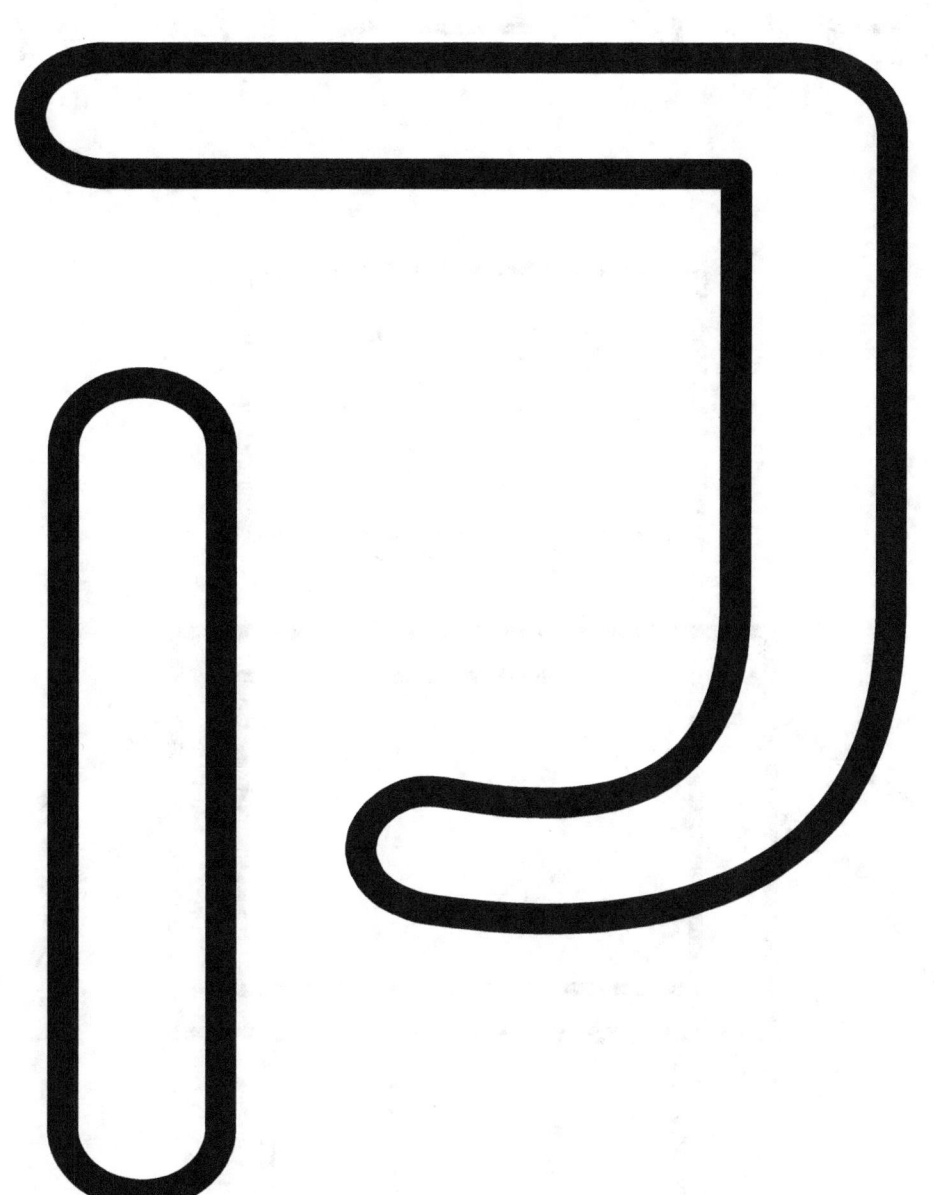

רובוט

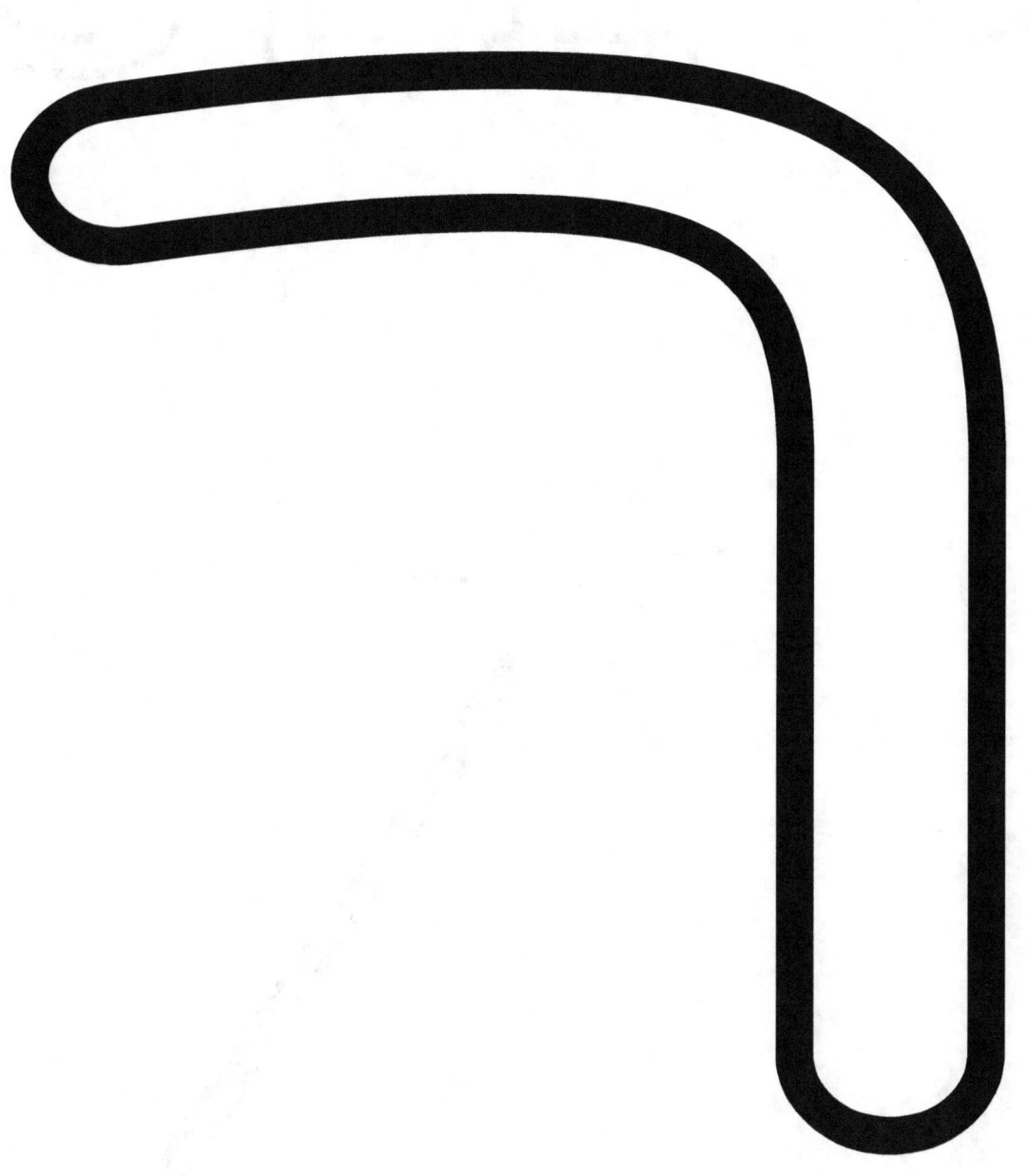

שרביט

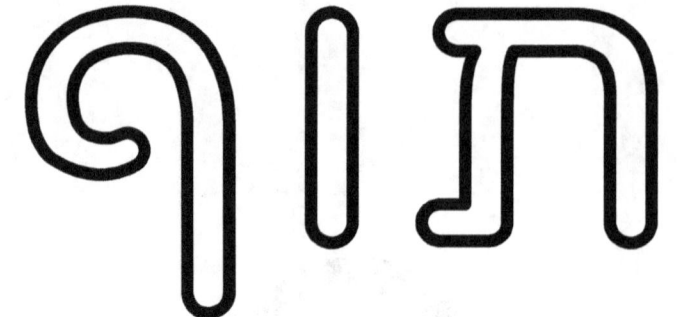

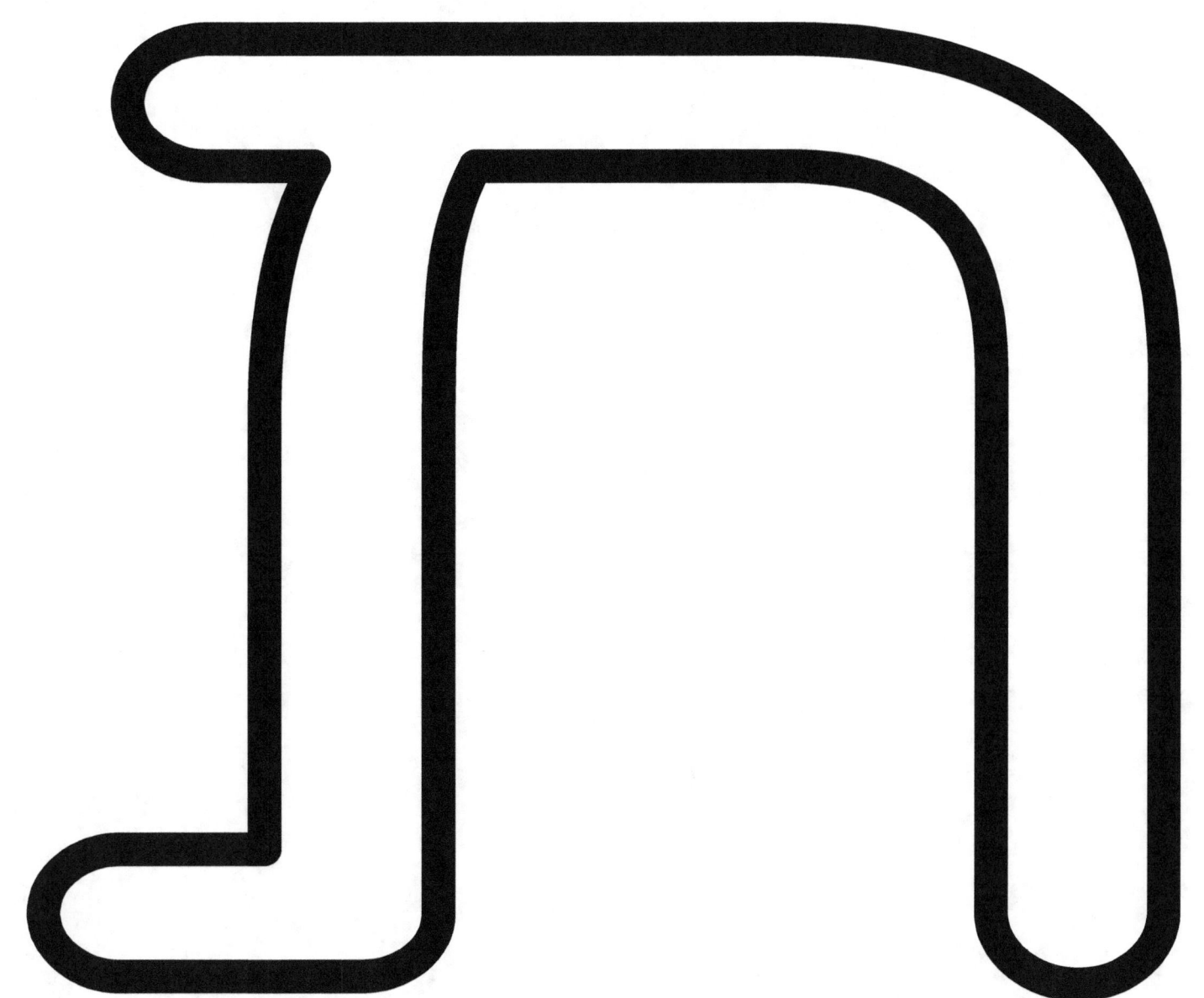

Also by Cactus Pear Books
Find more at cactuspearbooks.com

www.ingramcontent.com/pod-product-compliance
Lightning Source LLC
Chambersburg PA
CBHW081758100526
44592CB00015B/2481